BY MEGAN F. SALCH

Dedication
To the Frazier and Salch families,
who continue to give all they have to nurture all their children.
And to my loving husband for his support and humor.
Thanks for the memories.

Copyright © 2005 Tell Your Tale, LLC
Library of Congress Control Number: 2005909718
ISBN 0-9776154-0-5
All rights reserved, including the right of reproduction in whole or part in any form.
Book design and illustration by Debra Rohde and Robbie Short.
Edited by Roger Leslie.

I have selected the activities in this book based upon my family's experiences with these organizations. This is not an exhaustive list of available activities and omission of an activity does not necessarily imply the activity is not worthwhile. Individual preferences may vary and, thus, this book is intended to offer ideas for activities, not assurances that an activity will be perfect for any particular child. It is not a substitute for the individual judgment or exercise of responsible supervision by a parent or guardian.

D0898712

ATTENTiON PARENTS AND CAREGiVERS!

There are so many fun activities to do in Houston, but who has time to research them all? Welcome to **lOO+ ACTiVITiES** for Houston Kids - an easy way for local kids to maximize time with their parents and adult friends. Throw boredom out the window.

You can take advantage of seasonal activities easily because this book is categorized by the months of the year. However, many listings can be done throughout the year. Those activities are simply listed in a month to consider. Perhaps the location is least crowded during that month or maybe special discounts apply. Skim through the book to avoid missing anything.

For each listing, you will find a:
• category or type of activity (more than one may apply)
• description
• recommended age
• admission price
• physical location
• web site and/or phone number for more details and
• two grade boxes that allow a parent and a child to evaluate the activity
  based on letter grades given in school

CATEGORY LEGEND:

Art & Music

Charity/ Volunteer

History

Holiday

Nature

Parade

Science

Sports

I've made every effort to publish correct information on each activity, but dates, times and prices are subject to change. Call the organization to confirm the details before heading to your destination.

I hope that this book helps bring you and the children in your lives together through positive experiences. Take time today to plan your next activity and talk about what you enjoyed most. Play it month to month or skim through this annual book to find events that interest you and your children. Then, unleash the good times!

Hope to see you and your family around Houston!

Megan F. Salch

loo+ ACTIVITiES for Houston Kids

Start the New Year off right by finding a volunteer activity that you enjoy while helping others in this community. Visit www.volunteermatch.org and do an advanced search for activities that are great for kids in Houston. Find the activity that's right for you and sign up with a friend or make some new ones.

Recommended age: 3+ years
Admission: none
Physical location: depends on volunteer activity chosen
www.volunteermatch.org
How would you rate this? ☐ ☐

Each Friday and Saturday morning at 11:45 a.m., the Angelika Film Center presents **The Cry Baby Matinee at the Angelika** for parents all over Houston. Relax and enjoy a film at the Angelika without worrying about breastfeeding in the dark or squelching unexpected hissyfits. The theater dims the lights (rather than turns them off), lowers the volume, and rolls the film. The theater even provides changing tables at the front of the auditorium for diaper changing during the shows. This is a perfect outing when the weather outside is less than ideal, but appreciated year-round. An added bonus: the theater is not packed with movie goers so you and your little one have plenty of space.

Recommended age: adults with children under 5 years
Admission: Adults $6; Children under 5 FREE.
Physical location: 510 Texas Avenue (at the corner of Smith)
www.angelikafilmcenter.com/houston/
713-CALL-AFC (713-225-5232)
How would you rate this? ☐ ☐

1/14: The **Houston Rockets** basketball team will host kids' night on this Saturday to celebrate the 11th birthday of team mascot Clutch. Six visiting NBA mascots from across the country will perform at halftime. Plus, the first 5,000 fans will receive a Clutch piggy bank FREE. Game time is 7:30 p.m. when the Rockets play the New Orleans Hornets.

Recommended age: 3+ years
Admission: Tickets range from $10 - $185
Physical location: Toyota Center at 1510 Polk Street in downtown Houston
www.rockets.com Buy tickets at 866-4HOUTIX (866-446-8849),
www.toyotacentertix.com or participating Randalls stores
How would you rate this? ☐ ☐

1/16: The Houston **Zoo** celebrates Martin Luther King, Jr. Day by offering free admittance all day! Grab a coat and enjoy the animals when it's not so hot in town.
Recommended age: 1+ years
Admission: None today
Physical location: 1513 N. MacGregor
www.houstonzoo.org 713-533-6500
How would you rate this? ☐ ☐

1/17 -1/29: Theatre Under The Stars (TUTS) presents ***Doctor Dolittle,*** the amusing story of the doctor who can talk to animals.
Recommended age: 3+ years
Admission: $25-$82 per person; tickets are on sale beginning 12/4/05.
Physical location: Hobby Center for the Performing Arts: Sarofim Hall, 800 Bagby
www.tuts.com 713-558-TUTS (713-558-8887)
How would you rate this? ☐ ☐

Many children don't return to school until mid-January, so what's a kid to do? **Moody Gardens** in Galveston offers wonderful options, no matter what the weather. Kids will enjoy the aquarium, where they may touch a live starfish and cheer on the performing seals. Or travel through Moody Garden's rainforest, where children can spy exotic birds flying from tree to tree as they chirp merrily. Many kids will also enjoy the bat cave, where they learn how bats hang upside down. If that's not enough, there's also the Discovery Pyramid, where guides share educational details on space craft. Children under 3 are admitted free, but there's not much they can engage in.
Recommended age: 3+ years
Admission: A day pass for $35 may be the best option to take advantage of it all.
Physical location: One Hope Boulevard in Galveston
www.moodygardens.org 800-582-4673
How would you rate this? ☐ ☐

1/26: Attend ***Movie Magic: The Science Behind the Movies*** at Galveston's Grand 1894 Opera House. This interactive show allows attendees to learn what it takes to produce a movie from the lighting and sound to the acting. Held on Thursday, choose either the 10 a.m. show or the 7 p.m. show.
Recommended age: 8+ years
Admission: $8 - $10
Physical location: 2020 Postoffice Street in Galveston
www.thegrand.com 409-765-1894 or 800-821-1894
How would you rate this? ☐ ☐

1/28: **Asian Festival at the Houston Zoo**. Enjoy traditional lion and peacock dances, Chinese folk music, and origami and martial arts demonstrations. Learn more about the Asian animal species that live at the Houston Zoo including Siberian tigers, red crowned cranes, Chinese alligators and more. All the attractions of the Houston Zoo Asian Festival are included in your zoo admission.
Recommended age: 1+ years
Admission: Adults $8.50; Senior citizens $5; Children (age 2-11) $4; Children under 2 years FREE.
Physical location: 1513 N. MacGregor
www.houstonzoo.org 713-533-6500
How would you rate this?

1/28: The **Alley Theatre** features **Family Night Out** as a chance for parents to see an Alley performance while their 6-10 year old children participate in a creative drama workshop. This evening showcases *Culture Clash in America* for parents. Reservations are required. Children must be checked in by 7:30 p.m. and performances begin at 8 p.m.
Recommended age: 6-10 years
Admission: $10/child with the purchase of a theatre ticket
Physical location: 615 Texas Avenue in downtown Houston
www.alleytheatre.org Tickets: 713-228-8421;
Questions: 713-228-9341 ext. 425
How would you rate this?

1/30: *Amber Brown is not A Crayon* is showing at Galveston's Grand 1894 Opera House at 10 a.m. This performance tells the tale of a young girl whose best friend moves away. The entertaining piece teaches kids about the value of friendship.
Recommended age: 7+ years
Admission: $8 - $10
Physical location: 2020 Postoffice Street in Galveston
www.thegrand.com 409-765-1894 or 800-821-1894
How would you rate this?

February 2006:

2/2: Galveston's Grand 1894 Opera House offers two showings of
The Berenstain Bears On Stage! based on the best-selling book series. Choose either the 10 a.m. or 7 p.m. performance this Thursday.
Recommended age: 4-7 years
Admission: $8 - $10
Physical location: 2020 Postoffice Street in Galveston
www.thegrand.com 409-765-1894 or 800-821-1894
How would you rate this?

2/11: *Happy Birthday, Mozart!* plays at the Houston Symphony. This hour-long performance takes traditional music and puts a kid-friendly twist on it. This is an ideal activity for parents and children to do together. Enjoy either the 10 a.m. or 11:30 a.m. performance. Hands-on activities are available in the lobby before the first show and following the second performance. This is part of the Time Warner Family Concerts series.

Recommended age: 4-10 years
Admission: Adults $15; Children $9
Physical location: courtyard level of Jones Hall at 615 Louisiana St.
in downtown
www.houstonsymphony.org/education 713-224-7575
How would you rate this? ☐ ☐

Climb Mount Everest and fly through Grand Canyon all in one sitting. The Wortham **IMAX Theatre** is a cinematic experience for kids young and old. Parents won't mind sitting through these movies. And you won't mind visiting it again and again. Visitors learn about various continents without needing a passport, and the travels are fun.

Recommended age: 5+ years
Admission: Adults $7; Children $5.
Physical location: in Houston Museum of Natural Science at
One Hermann Circle Dr.
www.hmns.org 713-639-4629
How would you rate this? ☐ ☐

The **Planetarium** at the Houston Museum of Natural Science offers a nice break from the norm. Some shows are for more mature audiences, but kids 6-10 will enjoy shows such as *Legends of the Night Sky: Orion.* Unlike IMAX, the Planetarium features shows that are related to the museum's exhibits. Even space shuttle astronauts visit the planetarium for training purposes. Some children are scared once the lights go out, so be sure to reassure your children.

Recommended age: 6-10 years
Admission: Adults $6; children $4
Physical location: in Houston Museum of Natural Science at
One Hermann Circle Dr.
www.hmns.org 713-639-4629
How would you rate this? ☐ ☐

2/24: Galveston's Grand 1894 Opera House will feature ***The Civil War: The South Carolina Black Regiment*** at 10 a.m. Friday. This production combines music and history to tell the story of a young African American's search for freedom.
Recommended age: 8+ years
Admission: $8 - $10
Physical location: 2020 Postoffice Street in Galveston
www.thegrand.com 409-765-1894 or 800-821-1894
How would you rate this? ☐ ☐

2/25 in Houston means it's time for the downtown **Rodeo Parade,** 10 a.m. – 1 p.m. Chuck wagons, horses, and real cowboys and cowgirls have trotted their way to this rodeo for more than 65 years. This is a wonderful experience for the kids in your family. Dress up in your favorite denim and head downtown, but bring a blanket or jackets for the little ones since it's often cool outside this time of year.
Recommended age: All
Admission: No charge to watch the parade but parking fees may apply
Physical location: The route begins at Texas and Smith in downtown Houston, ending at Walker and Bagby.
www.hlsr.com/parade 832-667-1000
How would you rate this? ☐ ☐

2/18-2/19; 2/24-2/26: Be sure to take advantage of the **Mardi Gras** parades in Galveston. This is fun for the whole family as kids of all ages love seeing the festive floats and costumes. Get in on the action by catching beads, cups and more. All parades are publicly accessible, but the second weekend of Mardi Gras (2/24-2/26) requires paid admission to be on the Strand. Galveston is lowering ticket prices this year and you can purchase tickets in advance. Here are two kid-friendly parades to check out.
• Saturday, 2/18: *The Krewe of Aquarius* will hold its parade on the seawall beginning at noon. This is a great parade for the entire family.
• Sunday, 2/26: *The Childrens Parade* begins at 2 p.m. on 25th Street.
Recommended age: All ages. Bring strollers for young children.
Admission: No fee to attend the parades.
Physical location: various
www.mardigrasgalveston.com 888-GAL-ISLE (888-425-4753)
How would you rate this? ☐ ☐

2/26, 3/4 and 3/6: The **Houston Ballet** performs the favorite *Swan Lake* in matinee shows that delight children. This is a well-known love story of a prince who must choose a bride. The prince struggles with his emotions of finding a suitable mate but finds true love in the end. Arrive early to be seated because once the show begins, you will struggle to find your seat in the dimmed theater.
Recommended age: 5+ years
Admission: Tickets begin at $17
Physical location: Brown Theater at Wortham Theater Center at 501 Texas Avenue near Smith St.
www.houstonballet.org 713-523-6300
How would you rate this? ☐ ☐

2/28 – 3/19: Of course, we have the **Houston Livestock Show and Rodeo,** which is like no other rodeo nationwide. Matinee performances offer children a chance to see bull riders, barrel racers and famous performers ranging in music style from country to rock. But there's so much more than the rodeo itself. This is a great family activity. The outdoor carnival presents fun rides, games, and tasty treats. *Destination: AGventure* is an educational exhibit about… you guessed it… agriculture. Don't forget the petting zoo that features chickens, goats, ducks and much more. And rodeo visitors can view art work from local students to see some real talent. The pig races and pony rides are wonderful treasures.

Recommended age: All
Admission: Rodeo performance tickets begin at $17. The FunPass! costs $20 and gives you access to everything except the rodeo/concert activities for all 20 days of rodeo.
Physical location: Reliant Stadium and Reliant Park at 1 Reliant Park
www.hlsr.com/parade 832-667-1000
How would you rate this? ☐ ☐

Visit the Children's Museum of Houston February through May to see **Access-Ability** about people with handicaps. This exhibit features positive messages about how people can overcome handicaps and lead rewarding lives.

Recommended age: 3+ years
Admission: $5; Thursdays 5-8 p.m. are FREE; $3 Tuesday – Sunday 3-5 p.m.
Physical location: 1500 Binz in the Museum District
www.cmhouston.org 713-522-1138
Note: Open Tuesday - Saturday 9 a.m.- 5 p.m.; Sunday noon - 5 p.m. Only open on Mondays (9 a.m.- 5 p.m.) during the summer and federal holidays.
How would you rate this? ☐ ☐

3/1: Galveston's Grand 1894 Opera House hosts the production of **Danny, King of the Basement** at 10 a.m. This performance is the fun-loving tale of a boy who has learned to make friends easily because he has moved many times. This show encourages children to welcome newcomers and make new friends.
Recommended age: 8+ years
Admission: $8 - $10
Physical location: 2020 Postoffice Street in Galveston
www.thegrand.com 409-765-1894 or 800-821-1894
How would you rate this?

3/2: Dr. Seuss' Birthday is today so head to the **library** to read one of his hilariously fun tales. With so many books to choose from, you may find yourself spending an hour or more reading several tales.
Recommended age: 2+ years
Admission: None
Physical location: various
www.houstonlibrary.org 832-393-1313
How would you rate this?

3/2: **Broadway Jr** takes center stage at Galveston's Grand 1894 Opera House. By introducing young audiences to Broadway classics, this production is a delight to the ears. Choose from a 10 a.m. or 7 p.m. performance.
Recommended age: 7-10 years
Admission: $8 - $10
Physical location: 2020 Postoffice Street in Galveston
www.thegrand.com 409-765-1894 or 800-821-1894
How would you rate this?

3/12, 3/18 and 3/19: **Dance the World Round** is another production by the **Houston Ballet.** This production includes three separate ballets. The main performance is choreographed by Christopher Bruce specifically for the Houston Ballet. The second ballet is "Indigo"—a powerful, athletic piece. Finally, George Balanchine's "Western Symphony" is a light-hearted dance that highlights the American West with cowboys, saloon girls and more. Arrive early to be seated because once the show begins, you will struggle to find your seat in the dimmed theater.
Recommended age: 5+ years
Admission: Tickets begin at $17
Physical location: Brown Theater at Wortham Theater Center at 501 Texas Avenue near Smith St.
www.houstonballet.org 713-523-6300
How would you rate this?

3/13-3/19: Head to the Children's Museum of Houston this week for a head check. **Brain Awareness Week** features information on how we use our brains to interpret things such as optical illusions and brain teasers. The museum also focuses on logic and problem solving skills this week.
Recommended age: 3+ years
Admission: $5; Thursdays 5-8 p.m. are FREE; $3 Tuesday – Sunday 3-5 p.m.
Physical location: 1500 Binz in the Museum District
www.cmhouston.org 713-522-1138
Note: Open Tuesday - Saturday 9 a.m.- 5 p.m.; Sunday noon - 5 p.m.
Only open on Mondays (9 a.m.- 5 p.m.) during the summer and
federal holidays.
How would you rate this?

3/14 – 3/26: TUTS presents Disney's ***Beauty and the Beast.*** Enjoy the adventure of Belle and friends in this popular hit.
Recommended age: 3+ years
Admission: $25 - $82 per person; Tickets go on sale 12/4/05.
Physical location: Hobby Center for the Performing Arts: Sarofim Hall,
800 Bagby
www.tuts.com 713-558-TUTS (713-558-8887)
How would you rate this?

3/18: The **Alley Theatre** again features **Family Night Out** as a chance for parents to see an Alley performance while their 6-10 year old children participate in a creative drama workshop. For parents, this evening showcases *Born Yesterday* starring Oscar-winner Marisa Tomei. Reservations are required. Children must be checked in by 7:30 p.m. and performances begin at 8 p.m.
Recommended age: 6-10 years
Admission: $10/child with the purchase of a theatre ticket
Physical location: 615 Texas Avenue in downtown Houston
www.alleytheatre.org Tickets: 713-228-8421;
Questions: 713-228-9341 ext. 425
How would you rate this?

3/18: Wishing you the luck of the Irish! Get dressed in green for **Houston's Saint Patrick's Day Parade,** 2-4 p.m. With no admission cost, this is an entertaining Saturday afternoon for family and friends. Bring a wagon for youngsters to sit in.
Recommended age: All
Admission: No charge to watch parade but parking fees may apply
Physical location: The route begins at Texas and Hamilton in downtown
Houston, ending at Fannin and McKinney.

www.publicworks.cityofhouston.gov/traffic/events.htm
713-666-3601 x113
How would you rate this?

3/24-3/26: **The Bayou City Art Festival** has been rated one of the top 200 events in the United States. Don't miss this annual event. Enjoy the park's beauty while mingling with 300 local artists. Kids' activities include hat painting, sand blasting, jewelry making and more. This is a rain or shine event.

Recommended age: 3+ years
Admission: Adults $8; Children under 12 free.
Physical location: Memorial Park in central Houston (5 miles from downtown)
www.bayoucityartfestival.com 713-521-0133
How would you rate this? ☐ ☐

3/29: The **Alley Theatre** celebrates another **Family Night Out** as a chance for parents to see an Alley performance, while their 6-10 year old children participate in a creative drama workshop. For parents, this evening showcases *The Miser*. Reservations are required. Children must be checked in by 7:30 p.m. and performances begin at 8 p.m.
Recommended age: 6-10 years
Admission: $10/child with the purchase of a theatre ticket
Physical location: 615 Texas Avenue in downtown Houston
www.alleytheatre.org Tickets: 713-228-8421;
Questions: 713-228-9341 ext. 425
How would you rate this? ☐ ☐

April 2006:

4/1: April Fools Day – Take a trip to one of Houston's **parks** and just fool around. The weather in April tends to be nice (although it can change so quickly). For a list of city parks with a map, visit www.houstontx.gov/parks/.

Recommended age: 1+ year
Admission: FREE
Physical location: various locations throughout Houston
www.houstontx.gov/parks/ 713-845-1000
How would you rate this? ☐ ☐

4/1: Now here is a real treat. The **Grand Kid's Festival** from 10 a.m. – 5 p.m. is a fantastic way for parents and grandparents to spend time with their young children. Families enjoy three blocks of downtown Galveston festivities. Plus, the production of ***Robin Hood*** will be performed at 11 a.m. and 1:30 p.m.
Recommended age: 3+ years
Admission: $8 - $10
Physical location: 2020 Postoffice Street in Galveston
www.thegrand.com 409-765-1894 or 800-821-1894
How would you rate this? ☐ ☐

■ Take me out to the ballgame. **Minute Maid Park** is a wonder to see and offers something for everyone. Arrive early to take advantage of giveaways on special game days. Watch the retractable roof on this ballpark. And cheer on the Astros as the train sounds its horn when the Astros score. Join the Coca-Cola Astros Buddies Club for $10 per year and maximize your Astros spirit. Club membership entitles you to coupons for special Astros Buddies game days and Astros garb. Go 'Stros!

Recommended age: 2+ years

Admission: $1+ for children; $5+ for adults

Physical location: 501 Crawford Street in downtown Houston

www.astros.com/kids 713-259-8978

How would you rate this? ☐ ☐

■ Sundays Are Family Days at the **Museum of Fine Arts Houston** (MFAH). Kids and adults enjoy learning about art through Creation Station, a drop-in studio workshop. Families make their own paintings, sculpture, prints, photographs and more. Storytelling in the Galleries links art and literature for children, and provides an opportunity for children to create art after hearing stories.

Recommended age: 5+ years

Admission: Children $3.50; Adults $7; Children age 6-18 who show a Houston Public Library Power Card, Harris County Public Library Card, or any other Public Library Card are admitted FREE on Saturdays and Sundays. Thursdays are FREE for all.

Physical location: 1001 Bissonnet Street

www.mfah.org 713-639-7300

How would you rate this? ☐ ☐

■ Spring has sprung at **The Cockrell Butterfly Center** at the Houston Museum of Natural Science. See beautifully colored butterflies from around the globe and visit the Insect Zoo, too. Kids must be old enough to walk on their own because strollers are not allowed.

Recommended age: 2+ years

Admission: Adults $6; Children $4.

Physical location: One Hermann Circle Drive

www.hmns.org/ 713-639-4629

How would you rate this? ☐ ☐

4/15: ***Dr. Seuss's Gertrude McFuzz*** takes place at the Houston Symphony as an original musical based on the book of the same name. This performance lasts just under an hour so kids stay tuned in. The conductor is lively and speaks directly to the children, making the experience an entertaining one indeed. Enjoy either the 10 a.m. or 11:30 a.m. performance. Hands-on activities are available in the lobby before the first show and following the second performance. This is part of the Time Warner Family Concerts series.

Recommended age: 4-10 years
Admission: Adults $15; Children $9
Physical location: courtyard level of Jones Hall at 615 Louisiana St.
in downtown
www.houstonsymphony.org/education 713-224-7575
How would you rate this?

4/22: **Houston Ballet's Ben Stevenson Academy Spring Performance** will be held at 2:30 p.m. Attendees will see tomorrow's stars dance in productions designed specifically for them. Arrive early to be seated.

Recommended age: 5+ years
Admission: Tickets begin at $17
Physical location: Brown Theater at Wortham Theater Center at 501 Texas
Avenue near Smith St.
www.houstonballet.org 713-523-6300
How would you rate this?

4/25: **Discoverer Concerts** at the Houston Symphony is scheduled for 9:30 a.m. This is a fine way for school classes and other groups to learn history through music. Attendees will travel through experiences from the dinosaurs to the Liberty Bell. Concerts last approximately 50 minutes. Class or group leaders should contact the symphony to reserve group entrance.

Recommended age: 8-10 years
Admission: Children $4 with one free adult permitted for every 10
paid children
Physical location: courtyard level of Jones Hall at 615 Louisiana St.
in downtown
www.houstonsymphony.org/education/index.aspx 713-224-7575
How would you rate this?

5/2: The Houston Symphony's **Lollipop Concerts** will be held at 9:30 a.m. and 11:15 a.m. This concert series is geared for young audiences associated with elementary schools or clubs. This year's theme is Sherlock Holmes as children listen to musical clues in hopes of solving the *Case of the Missing Orchestra.* Concerts last approximately 50 minutes. Class or group leaders should contact the symphony to reserve group entrance.
Recommended age: 4-9 years
Admission: Children $4 with one free adult permitted for every 10 paid children
Physical location: courtyard level of Jones Hall at 615 Louisiana St. in downtown
www.houstonsymphony.org/education/index.aspx 713-224-7575
How would you rate this?

5/4 is Space Day so drive south of Houston to the **Challenger Learning Center** at George Observatory, which is located in Brazos Bend State Park. Kids in first grade and up can explore space simulation or view solar flares through the telescopes. This is great for your young astronaut-to-be. The observatory is open Saturdays 3 p.m. - 10 p.m.
Recommended age: 6+ years
Admission: $5/person for all three telescopes and presentations
Physical location: Brazos Bend State Park, 1 hour from downtown Houston
www.hmns.org/see_do/george_observatory.asp 281-242-3055
How would you rate this?

5/5: Ready to travel? Head to the **Children's Museum of Houston** on Cinco de Mayo to learn about the culture of Mexico. Visit the simulated Mexican village of Yalalag, where kids can barter for goods and learn Zapotec words as they explore the kid-sized town. Walk through the Zocalo to shop for food in the open-air market, take a ride on the VW bus, and see vivid photographs and authentic folk art from this town. Call ahead to inquire about the time of the live mariachi band.
Recommended age: 3+ years
Admission: $5; Thursdays 5-8 p.m. are FREE; $3 Tuesday – Sunday 3-5 p.m.
Physical location: 1500 Binz in the Museum District
www.cmhouston.org 713-522-1138
Note: Open Tuesday - Saturday 9 a.m.- 5 p.m.; Sunday noon - 5 p.m.
Only open on Mondays (9 a.m.- 5 p.m.) during the summer and federal holidays.
How would you rate this?

5/9 – 5/21: TUTS presents ***110 in the Shade,*** which is based on the famous play *The Rainmaker.* This children's feature introduces Lizzie as the main character who meets an entertaining stranger full of outlandish promises. Audiences revel in the tale as Lizzie questions whether this stranger is truly magical.
Recommended age: 3+ years
Admission: $25-$82 per person; Tickets go on sale 3/12/06.
Physical location: Hobby Center for the Performing Arts: Sarofim Hall, 800 Bagby
www.tuts.com 713-558-TUTS (713-558-8887)
How would you rate this?

5/12: Kite Day: head to a city park and teach your child how to **fly a kite.** Is your child old enough? Typically, children who can hold onto a balloon without accidentally releasing it can also fly a kite with some guidance. Bring along a bottle of bubbles for those younger children to enjoy.
Recommended age: ~3+ years for kite flying; 6+ months to enjoy bubbles
Admission: None
Physical location: various
www.houstontx.gov/parks 713-845-1000
How would you rate this?

5/13: Load the kids in a wagon and head to **Everyones Art Car Parade** on Allen Parkway. Parade viewers see creativity at its finest with cars decorated in off-beat ways as well as a few classics. Kids of all ages enjoy the sights and sounds of this line up. Pack some sandwiches and drinks to enjoy during the procession. And don't forget the Art Car Parade Awards Ceremony and Brunch on Sunday, May 14, which is very family-friendly and fun.
Recommended age: ~1+ years
Admission: None
Physical location: Allen Parkway near downtown
www.orangeshow.org 713-926-6368
How would you rate this?

5/19-5/21: Known as the "Home of the World's Largest Strawberry Shortcake," the **Strawberry Festival** offers a wide variety of food, arts and crafts, activities and entertainment for the whole family to enjoy. Children 3 months to 8 years may compete in the Baby Parade contest, too. Guests also enjoy a petting zoo, pony rides, circus activities and more.
Recommended age: All
Admission: Adults $8; Students with Student ID: $5; Children Under 12: $4; Children under 5 free
Physical location: Pasadena Convention Center and Municipal Fairgrounds at 7902 Fairmont Parkway at Red Bluff Road in Pasadena.
www.strawberryfest.org 281-991-9500
How would you rate this?

5/28 and 6/4: Kids can groove to **Houston Ballet's *Classical x 3,*** three classical ballet performances set to the techno dance music of Moby. First, Stanton Welch's "Play" is an extraordinary take on busy urban life. Next, youngsters enjoy Sir Kenneth MacMillan's "Gloria" — performed in only a few cities worldwide. Finally, "Velocity" uses fast dance moves by young and athletic dancers. Arrive early to be seated because once the show begins, you will struggle to find your seat in the dimmed theater.
Recommended age: 5+ years
Admission: Tickets begin at $17
Physical location: Brown Theater at Wortham Theater Center at 501 Texas Avenue near Smith St.
www.houstonballet.org 713-523-6300
How would you rate this?

5/31: Memorial Day – Enjoy a free day at the **Houston Zoo!** What a fun way to start your summer.
Recommended age: 1+ years
Admission: None today
Physical location: 1513 N. MacGregor
www.houstonzoo.org 713-533-6500
How would you rate this?

When the kids are out of school, head to **Space Center Houston** for activities that are both educational and fun. Young visitors will enjoy the Kids Space Place, which features kid-sized astronaut equipment and lots of hands-on activities. Other astronauts-at-heart will love this place for the tram tours of the Johnson Space Center, interactive exhibits and more. Allow for five hours to take advantage of everything.
(Spring, summer and fall feature different children's exhibits so visit again to see the changing displays.)
Recommended age: 6+ years
Admission: Adults $18; Children (age 4-11) $14. See The Houston Chronicle for 50 percent off coupons. Parking is an additional $4.
Physical location: 1601 NASA Road 1, approximately 25 miles south of downtown Houston in the NASA/Clear Lake area
www.spacecenter.org 281-244-2100
How would you rate this?

Texans Youth Football Camps take place in June and July. Football players, age 8-14, are instructed by top-area high school coaches on the fundamentals of football in a program designed for beginners and experienced players. Athletes age 8-14 learn flag football while older kids try out tackle football. The camp includes visits and autographs from Texans players each day. All participants receive a camp jersey, four FREE training camp tickets and other great Texans giveaways. Plus, adult football fans will love hearing stories about the NFL players who guide their kids.
Recommended age: 8-14 years
Admission: TBD
Physical location: Texans Practice Facility
www.HoustonTexans.com
E-mail youthfootball@houstontexans.com
How would you rate this?

The Children's Museum of Houston showcases the **Alice's Wonderland** exhibit based on the book *Alice in Wonderland*. This traveling exhibit is available through September so beat the heat by heading inside.
Recommended age: 3+ years
Admission: $5; Thursdays 5-8 p.m. are FREE; $3 Tuesday – Sunday 3-5 p.m.
Physical location: 1500 Binz in the Museum District
www.cmhouston.org 713-522-1138
Note: Open Tuesday - Saturday 9 a.m.- 5 p.m.; Sunday noon - 5 p.m.
Only open on Mondays (9 a.m.- 5 p.m.) during the summer and federal holidays.
How would you rate this?

6/3: Enjoy the **Alley Theatre Family Night Ou**t as a chance for parents to see an Alley performance while their 6-10 year old children participate in a creative drama workshop. For parents, this evening showcases *Witness for the Prosecution*. Reservations are required. Children must be checked in by 7:30 p.m. and performances begin at 8 p.m.
Recommended age: 6-10 years
Admission: $10/child with the purchase of a theatre ticket
Physical location: 615 Texas Avenue in downtown Houston
www.alleytheatre.org Tickets: 713-228-8421;
Questions: 713-228-9341 ext. 425
How would you rate this?

6/3: The **AIA Sandcastle Competition** in Galveston heats up this Saturday. Have fun looking at the wonders that folks create in the sand and gain some inspiration for your own sandcastle. Bring a backpack carrier for young kids and wear sandals or flip flops that allow the sand to easily empty from your shoes.
Recommended age: All
Admission: Free event. Parking is $5 per entry.
Physical location: East Beach in Galveston
www.aiasandcastle.com 713-520-0155
How would you rate this?

When the heat is unbearable in Houston, tackle some indoor activity by **roller skating.** The need for balance leads to a hilarious bonding experience for adults and children. Several rinks are around town but two options are listed below for your convenience.

• Dairy Ashford Roller Rink
Recommended age: 3+ years
Admission: $4.25 - $5.50, depending on day and time
Physical location: 1820 S Dairy Ashford St.;
281-493-5651
This location offers a Preschool Skate program for children 6 and under (and their parents) every Friday.
How would you rate this?

• Airline Skate Center
Recommended age: 5+ years
Admission: $3 and up, depending on day and time
Physical location: 10715 Airline Dr.
www.airlineskatecenter.com/ 281-448-7845
How would you rate this?

The Houston Symphony invites families to participate in the **Sounds Like Fun!** series throughout the month of June. Entertain and educate young audiences with the FREE concerts throughout Houston neighborhoods. Enjoy an hour performance with themes that delight children's ears.
Recommended age: 4-10 years
Admission: FREE
Physical location: 15 performances covering the Greater Houston area
www.houstonsymphony.org/education/index.aspx 713-238-1449
E-mail e&o@houstonsymphony.com
How would you rate this?

6/11, 6/17 and 6/18: Is there a ballerina in your house? Then dance to the **Houston Ballet.** The troupe performs the love story set in Spain entitled *Don Quixote.* Arrive early to be seated because once the show begins, you will struggle to find your seat in the dimmed theater.
Recommended age: 5+ years
Admission: Tickets begin at $17
Physical location: Brown Theater at Wortham Theater Center at 501 Texas Avenue near Smith St.
www.houstonballet.org 713-523-6300
How would you rate this? ☐ ☐

Since June is aquarium month, be sure to visit the **Downtown Aquarium,** which is a true delight. The numerous aquarium exhibits amaze children of all ages. For a short visit, head to the Downtown Aquarium restaurant, where visitors can view sting rays, eels and more while eating a meal. A kids menu with coloring activities is an added bonus.

If your group has an afternoon or more, enjoy all that this attraction offers. Besides the amazing aquarium itself, kids can also enjoy an educational train ride around the park, various amusement park rides (including the 100-foot ferris wheel), and games. Tip: bring a change of clothes or swim suit so your little ones can play in the dancing fountain at the entrance to the rides and enjoy the mister on a hot day.
Recommended Age: 3+ years
Admission: Pay $16 to take advantage of the aquarium and all rides, instead of paying individual ticket prices.
Physical location: 410 Bagby St. and Memorial Dr. in downtown Houston
www.downtownaquariumhouston.com or call 713-223-FISH (3474).
How would you rate this? ☐ ☐

The **Milky Way Play Castle** is a big hit with kids at Memorial City Mall on the west side of Houston. This is a good way to beat the Houston heat or have fun on a rainy day. This colorful playground measures 21 feet high and includes a slide, bridge, crawling tunnels, a pretend moat and mushroom-like stepping stones. Seats around the perimeter are available for adults. Conveniently park your stroller within the castle grounds. The play castle is open daily during mall hours and allows young children to kick off their shoes and roam freely.
Recommended age: 48" tall maximum; 1+ year
Admission: FREE
Physical location: Memorial City Mall at I-10 and Gessner
How would you rate this? ☐ ☐

- Another inexpensive activity in Memorial City Mall is riding the **Carousel.** Located on the south side of the mall near the food court, the two-level carousel is quite a fantasy. After a short trip around, grab a bite to eat from one of the many restaurants nearby.
Recommended age: 36" tall minimum to ride without a guardian; Children under 36" tall may ride with an accompanying guardian, who rides for free.
Admission: $1
Physical location: Memorial City Mall at I-10 and Gessner
How would you rate this? ☐ ☐

- Head indoors for some fun at a **Build-A-Bear Workshop**®. Children can design their own bear or other critter and learn the process of making that stuffed animal. Participants stuff the fuzzy animals, make hearts for the loved ones, print birth certificates, and select a miniature house (a take-home box) for the newborn animal.
Recommended age: 5+ years
Admission: $10-$25 for a bear or critter + optional accessories; under $40 total
Physical location: Galleria Mall at 5085 Westheimer Road, #3605; 713-355-3388
Memorial City Mall located near Gessner and I-10; 713-468-6987
www.buildabear.com
How would you rate this? ☐ ☐

- **Oil Ranch** is a fun trip out of the city with so much to do for the entire family. Plan on spending a good part of your day here to allow for the drive and all the activities. With lifeguards provided, the swimming pool is open during the summer through September, so bring your swimsuits. Other activities include pony rides, playing among Indian teepees, touring the lake by train and more. Be sure to milk a cow the old fashioned way. It's really something to experience. Operating hours depend on the time of year, so call ahead to make reservations.
Recommended age: 2+ years
Admission: $9 per person; Discounts are available for groups of 10 or more.
Physical location: #1 Oil Ranch Road in Hockley.
From Houston, head northwest on 610. Take Highway 290 West. Exit Hegar Rd. (Hegar Rd. is approx. 16 miles west of 1960/Hwy. 6 on 290 and 29 miles from the 610 loop). Turn right on Hegar Rd. Go approximately 5 miles and follow the signs to the Oil Ranch.
www.oilranch.com 281-859-1616
How would you rate this? ☐ ☐

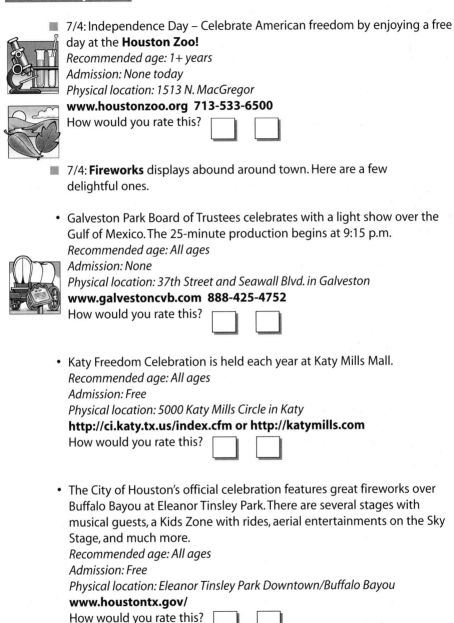

■ 7/4: Independence Day – Celebrate American freedom by enjoying a free
day at the **Houston Zoo!**
Recommended age: 1+ years
Admission: None today
Physical location: 1513 N. MacGregor
www.houstonzoo.org 713-533-6500
How would you rate this?

■ 7/4: **Fireworks** displays abound around town. Here are a few
delightful ones.

• Galveston Park Board of Trustees celebrates with a light show over the
Gulf of Mexico. The 25-minute production begins at 9:15 p.m.
Recommended age: All ages
Admission: None
Physical location: 37th Street and Seawall Blvd. in Galveston
www.galvestoncvb.com 888-425-4752
How would you rate this?

• Katy Freedom Celebration is held each year at Katy Mills Mall.
Recommended age: All ages
Admission: Free
Physical location: 5000 Katy Mills Circle in Katy
http://ci.katy.tx.us/index.cfm or http://katymills.com
How would you rate this?

• The City of Houston's official celebration features great fireworks over
Buffalo Bayou at Eleanor Tinsley Park. There are several stages with
musical guests, a Kids Zone with rides, aerial entertainments on the Sky
Stage, and much more.
Recommended age: All ages
Admission: Free
Physical location: Eleanor Tinsley Park Downtown/Buffalo Bayou
www.houstontx.gov/
How would you rate this?

Since July is National Picnic Month, why not pack a lunch and head to **Williams Tower and Waterwall?** Children love to see the water pouring over the edge of this super tall creation. Make guesses as to how much water there is and why it makes so much noise. Then, enjoy a picnic while you soak in the view. Don't forget your camera. This makes a great backdrop for some family photos.

Recommended age: All ages
Admission: Free
Physical location: 2800 Post Oak Blvd. near the Galleria
713-966-7799
How would you rate this? ☐ ☐

Cool off with ice cream at the **Blue Bell Creamery** in Brenham, Texas. Okay, so it's outside Houston, but it's too tasty to miss. Hungry? Tours last 45 minutes and are scheduled throughout the day Monday – Friday, 10 a.m., 11 a.m., 1 p.m., 1:30 p.m. and 2 p.m. Each tour ends with a tasty treat of ice cream. Yummy!

Recommended age: 2+ years
Admission: Adults = $3; Senior Citizens and Kids 6-14 $2; Kids under 6 free.
Physical location: 1101 South Horton in Brenham, TX. From Houston, take Hwy. 290 to Brenham. Turn right on FM 577 and continue 2 miles.
www.BlueBell.com 979-836-7977
How would you rate this? ☐ ☐

7/29: The Houston Zoo kicks off **Operation School Supplies.** This is a school supplies drive as part of a citywide effort to raise $150,000 in school supplies for needy elementary students. From 9 a.m. - 1 p.m., the zoo will give a child's admission ticket to every child that donates school supplies.

Recommended age: 1+ years
Admission: School supply donation instead of regular ticket price
Physical location: 1513 N. MacGregor
www.houstonzoo.org 713-533-6500
How would you rate this? ☐ ☐

Capture the essence of summer when you **pick your own watermelon** fresh from the vine. Kids love to eat what they pick. This is a great way to learn how fruit and vegetables grow. Visit www.agr.state.tx.us/picktexas/index.htm to find a farm near you. In addition to watermelon, you can pick blueberries, blackberries and more.

Recommended age: 3+ years
Admission: varies by farm
Physical location: varies
www.agr.state.tx.us/picktexas/index.htm
How would you rate this? ☐ ☐

When your family is climbing the walls, head to **Texas Rock Gym** and put that energy to good use. For youngsters, top-rope climbing is your best bet. This requires two people: a climber and a belayer. The adult can best serve as the belayer, who stays on the ground to operate the safety equipment and keep the climber's rope taut. This way, if the climber lets go or falls, they won't go far. Then, the climber can focus his/her energy on climbing to the top of the mountain. Not only is this fun, but it also teaches kids health, discipline, trust (with the belayer) and confidence. Visits during off-peak hours allow you more time climbing and lower prices. Peak hours are Fridays 3 p.m. - Sunday 5 p.m.

Recommended age: 5+ years
Admission: Prices vary based on location but plan on approximately $24/person. The Clear Lake location is less expensive but is smaller. A $7.50 student (week)day pass is available only at the Clear Lake location.
Physical location: Memorial location is 1526 Campbell 713-973-7625
Clear Lake location is 201 Hobbs R.D., Suite #A1 in League City 281-338-7625
www.texrockgym.com/
How would you rate this? ☐ ☐

August 2006:

How about a cool way to cheer on good nutrition and fun art? The **Orange Show Monument** is an outdoor 3,000 square foot structure with maze-like design. It includes an oasis, a wishing well, a pond, a stage, a museum, a gift shop, and several upper decks. It is constructed of concrete, brick, steel and found objects including gears, tiles, wagon wheels, mannequins, tractor seats and statuettes. This is a family-fun way to embrace funky art that sings the praises of the orange, the favorite fruit of the monument's creator. The Orange Show Monument is open from 9 a.m. - 1 p.m. Wednesdays – Fridays during the summer months as well as weekends noon – 5 p.m. (You can also visit noon - 5 p.m. on the weekends between Labor Day and Memorial Day.)

Recommended age: All
Admission: $1/adult
Physical location: 2402 Munger St.
www.orangeshow.org 713-926-6368
How would you rate this? ☐ ☐

8/6: Friendship Day – Take your child and his/her friend to the Film Festival at the **Wortham IMAX Theatre** at the Houston Museum of Natural Science. The festival runs from mid-August to September each year and offers about eight different films. Visit the Web site for a listing of this year's films and costs.

Recommended age: 5+ years
Admission: Adults $7; Children $5
Physical location: One Hermann Circle Dr.
www.hmns.org 713-639-4629
How would you rate this?

8/11 is **Play in the Sand Day** so drive down to **Galveston** for some fun in the sun. Pack a lunch, drinks, beach towels, and sand toys for a day of entertainment. Don't forget your sun block. Beaches to try are: East Beach, Galveston Island State Park, Stewart Beach (includes a playground) and a few pocket beaches.

Recommended age: 1+ years
Admission: Fees begin at $3 depending upon which beach you visit.
Physical location: various
www.galveston.com 888-GAL-ISLE (888-425-4753)
How would you rate this?

Beat the heat by **ice skating.** This is a lot of fun and it's not often that Houstonians see ice. Classes and summer camps are also available for the cautious. Ready for a break? Watch the competitive skaters twirl on the ice. The ice rinks are open daily but hours vary.

Recommended age: 5+ years

• Polar Ice Galleria
Recommended age: 5+ years
Admission: Children under 12 $6.50, plus skate rental of $3
Physical location: within the Houston Galleria mall at 610 and Westheimer
www.polaricegalleria.com 713-621-1500
How would you rate this?

• Ice Skate USA
Admission: Adult $6.50 + $3 skate rental; Children under 10 and seniors $5.50 + $3 skate rental; Children 5 and under $3.50 (including skate rental)
Physical location: within Memorial City Mall located at I-10 and Gessner
**www.shopmemorialcity.com/dining_events/ice_skate.html
713-463-9296**
How would you rate this?

Get to know the roots of Houston by visiting **Allen's Landing.** This park on Buffalo Bayou marks the spot where the Allen brothers began the new town called Houston in 1836. Walk through some restored 19th-century buildings. Enjoy the small park amid the skyscrapers. Head out early to avoid the heat and then check out one of the great restaurants in Houston.

Recommended age: All.
Admission: Free.
Physical location: 1001 Commerce Street; bordered by Travis, Milam, Congress, and Preston St.
www.buffalobayou.org/allenslanding.html
How would you rate this? ☐ ☐

Visit the **Nolan Ryan Center** in Alvin in tribute of a hometown hero. Exhibits show the great pitcher's history from little league baseball through the majors. Youngsters love the pitch-catch exhibit that allows them to experience the feel of catching one of Ryan's pitches. The Center is open Tuesday-Saturday 9 a.m. – 4 p.m. and Sunday noon – 4 p.m. The Center is closed Mondays. Strollers are not permitted.

Recommended age: 5+ years
Admission: Adults $5; Children $2
Physical location: Alvin Community College at 2925 South Bypass 35
www.alvin.cc.tx.us/ryan/nolan.htm 281-388-1134
How would you rate this? ☐ ☐

September 2006:

Visit the Heights during the **Heights First Saturday** celebration to see local talent and enjoy a small town feeling within this big city. Browse various forms of art and jewelry and purchase a favorite. The Yale Street Arts Market is part of the Heights First Saturday event and includes many artists who create items just for children such as clothes, toys and decorations. Free trolley tours are available from 12:30 p.m. – 4 p.m. This event is held the first Saturday of each month from 9 a.m. – 5 p.m. Some Saturdays also include plays and puppet shows for children. What a fun way to get familiar with the Heights.

Recommended age: 6+ months
Admission: Free
Physical location: Trolley tour begins at Hickory Hollow Restaurant at 101 Heights Boulevard. The Yale Street Arts Market is located at 210 West 21st Street -- a block off Yale.
www.heightsfirstsaturday.com 713-802-1213
www.yalestreetmarket.com
How would you rate this? ☐ ☐

9/4: Labor Day – Take a break from work and enjoy a free day at the **Houston Zoo.**
Recommended age: 1+ years
Admission: None today
Physical location: 1513 N. MacGregor

www.houstonzoo.org 713-533-6500
How would you rate this? ☐ ☐

Everyone Counts opens this month at the Children's Museum of Houston and runs through December. This is a wonderful math exhibit that allows young visitors to learn while having fun. Then, become an artist at the museum's "Expressions" area, where painters get creative in an open-air studio.
Recommended age: 3+ years
Admission: $5; Thursdays 5-8 p.m. are free; $3 Tuesday – Sunday 3-5 p.m.
Physical location: 1500 Binz in the Museum District
www.cmhouston.org 713-522-1138
Note: Open Tuesday - Saturday 9 a.m.- 5 p.m.; Sunday noon - 5 p.m. Only open on Mondays (9 a.m.- 5 p.m.) during the summer and federal holidays.
How would you rate this? ☐ ☐

9/24 is **Good Neighbor Day** and no matter where you live, you can always help a neighbor. Bake some cookies for your neighbors or color a picture for them. Take them a potted plant or fresh-cut flowers. Brainstorm on the nice things you can do for neighbors and get started.
Recommended age: All
Admission: None
Physical location: your neighborhood

Enjoy a ferry ride by driving or walking aboard the **Galveston Island Ferry.** The ride covers 2.7 miles to Port Bolivar with views of the Bolivar Lighthouse and Seawolf Park. The ferry runs 24 hours a day and is a fun, free ride. Avoid the crowds by attending during the week in the summer or weekends of non-summer months.
Recommended age: All ages
Admission: Free
Physical location: End of Ferry Road in Galveston
409-763-2386
How would you rate this? ☐ ☐

Native Texans and transplants will enjoy a trip to the **Sam Houston Memorial Museum** north on I-45 in Huntsville. Learn more about Sam Houston, the first president of the Republic of Texas, while looking up at the 67 foot statue of this gentleman. The museum is open Tuesdays – Saturdays 9 a.m. – 4:30 p.m. and Sundays noon – 4:30 p.m.
Recommended age: 5+ years
Admission: Free
Physical location: corner of Sam Houston Avenue and 19th St. in Huntsville
www.shsu.edu/~smm_www/ 936-294-1832
How would you rate this?

Children love the **Houston Museum of Natural Science** for its wonderful exhibits. The dinosaurs are always a big hit, but don't miss the other exhibits focusing on Texas wildlife, gems and minerals, and much more. Adults can walk kids through the exhibits and explain what each describes. Children can then discuss their thoughts and reactions. The Fondren Discovery Place is an interactive, permanent exhibit for kids, so check that out, too.

Recommended age: 3+ years
Admission: Adults $7; Children $4.
Physical location: One Hermann Circle Drive
www.hmns.org/ 713-639-4629
How would you rate this?

The **Bayou Wildlife Park** in Alvin is a miniature safari for families to explore without traveling across time zones. Take a ride on the Exotic Tram to see the wildlife. Kids like the pony rides and petting zoo. The park is open March – October: 10a.m. - 4:30 p.m. Tuesday - Sunday; (From November – February, the park hours are 10 a.m. - 3:30 p.m. Tuesday – Sunday.)

Recommended age: 1+ year
Admission: Adults $9; Children $5.50
Physical location: 5050 FM 517 RD in Alvin
281-337-6376
How would you rate this?

The **Texas Renaissance Festival** runs on Saturdays and Sundays in October and November from 9 a.m. to dusk. As a fun family day, attendees can see 16th century costumes, cheer on jousting events, and enjoy festive food and music. Don't forget to see the glass blowing, make a candle of your own, and try your aim at archery.
Recommended age: 5+ years
Admission: Adults $21; Children $10. For discounts, purchase advance tickets. Games and rides are additional.
Physical location: From Houston, take I-45 north to Conroe. Exit Highway 105 west and turn left under the freeway. Follow Highway 105 approximately 20 miles to Plantersville. In Plantersville, turn left onto FM 1774 and go 6 miles to the festival entrance.
www.TexRenFest.com 800-458-3435
How would you rate this?

10/4: On **National Golf Day,** try some putt-putt golf with the family. Three venues are listed below but many are available throughout Houston. Plus, these entertainment centers also offer other games once your little golfer(s) yearns for other activities.
Recommended age: 2+ years

- Celebration Station
  Admission: Adults $6; Children 5-12 years $4; Children under 5 years free with paying adult
  Physical location: 180 West Rankin Rd., Houston 77090; 281-872-7778
  Physical location: 6767 Southwest Freeway, Houston 77074; 713-981-7888
  www.celebrationstation.com
  How would you rate this?

- Funplex
  Admission: Regularly adults $4; children $3.75; Fridays $0.99 for all
  Physical location: 13700 Beechnut, Houston 77083
  www.funplex.org 281-530-7777
  How would you rate this?

- Putting Edge Glow-in-the-Dark Mini Golf
  Admission: 13+ years $8.50; 7-12 years $7.50; 5-6 years and seniors $6; under 4 years free.
  Physical location: 7620 Katy Freeway in the Marq-E Entertainment Center
  www.puttingedge.com 713-263-7051
  How would you rate this?

10/7: **Race for the Cure** in Houston is a moving experience for folks of all ages. Even if you're not a runner, sign up to walk the Kids K/Family Walk event and bring a stroller for younger children. Kids who are ready to give it their all are encouraged to participate with their parents/guardians in the noncompetitive 5K. All registrants receive a T-shirt and big congratulations. Youth participants receive either a bib or youth T-shirt. The Post-Race party is also tons of fun. What a great way to encourage children to contribute to the community by raising money to support a worthy cause.

Recommended age: 6 months+
Admission: $30/adult and $10/child
Physical location: The 2005 location was changed from previous years due to the George R. Brown Convention Center becoming a shelter for Hurricane Katrina victims. Check the Web site for details on the 2006 route.
www.komen-houston.org
How would you rate this? ☐ ☐

10/20-10/22 and 10/27-10/29: Enjoy safe Halloween trick-or-treating fun with a "naturally wild" twist at **Zoo Boo's** "Main Events" from 4-8 p.m. Fridays and Saturdays, and 2-5 p.m. Sundays. This year, Zoo Boo features the kid-friendly "Happy Haunted House," an animal themed haunted house specially designed for little goblins 10 years of age and under with rooms created by seven local artists. Get in the spirit of Halloween with the Pumpkin Glow featuring 500 illuminated pumpkins each evening at the Zoo Reflection Pool, children's trick-or-treat and craft booths, costume parades and costume contests, special musical presentations, magic shows, and the stars of Zoo Boo—more that 3,100 animals from around the world. All Zoo Boo events are included in the regular price of admission.

Recommended age: 1+ years
Admission: Adults $8.50; Senior citizens $5; Children (age 2-11) $4; Children under 2 years free.
Physical location: 1513 N. MacGregor
www.houstonzoo.org 713-533-6500
How would you rate this? ☐ ☐

10/21: The Houston Fire Museum sponsors **Fire Fest** 2006 10 a.m. – 5 p.m. Bring the kids to enjoy fire demonstrations, fire trucks, music, food and fun. This is a great way for children to learn how the fire department serves Houstonians. Plus, children love to shake hands with real firefighters.

Recommended age: 3+ years
Admission: Free
Physical location: HFD Val Jahnke Training Facility at 8030 Braniff (off Telephone Rd. behind Hobby Airport)
www.houstonfiremuseum.org 713-524-2526
How would you rate this? ☐ ☐

10/29: The 24th annual Island **Oktoberfest** will be held Saturday 11 a.m. – 7 p.m. Enjoy German music, dancing, and tasty food. Children enjoy the pony carrousel, a trackless train, moon walks, rock climbing wall, a mechanical bull, face painting, and more.
Recommended age: All

Admission: Free
Physical location: First Evangelical Lutheran Church in Galveston at 24th and Winnie St.
www.1st.lutheran.com 409-762-8477
How would you rate this? ☐ ☐

A trip to **Farmers Market** is a treat any time of the year, but visits during cooler months are most enjoyable since there is no air conditioning. (There are some indoor/outdoor fans though.) Not only can adults get good deals on fresh fruit and vegetables from area farmers, but they can also use this as an opportunity to teach children how food arrives at the store by speaking with the local merchants. Plants and flowers are also available as well as seasonal items such as piñatas, pumpkins, etc. This is a stroller-friendly place. Avoid pushing a stroller and a shopping cart by bringing a large mesh bag to carry purchases. Wear cool, comfortable clothes. No checks accepted.
Recommended age: All ages
Admission: No cost to enter. Goods are marked for retail, but some vendors will barter.
Physical location: 2520 Airline near I-45 North
713-862-4027
How would you rate this? ☐ ☐

Take your crew to a local pumpkin patch to jumpstart a festive mood. Our family favorite is **Dewberry Farm.** This attraction features the "Punkin Patch," where visitors take a short hayride to fields of pumpkins to make their selection. Kids enjoy the corn field maze, a barn full of farm animals, and a musical show. Little Farmersville is a play area for kids six and under, which includes tricycles, old fashioned rocking horses, hay

stacks, and climbable tractor tires. Hours of operation are Friday 4-10 p.m.; Saturday 10 a.m.-9 p.m.; Sunday noon – dark. Bring a hat to keep the sun and sand out of your eyes when it's dusty and windy. Wear closed-toe shoes and jeans for maximum comfort. Dewberry Farm just may become a new October tradition for your family, too.
Recommended age: All ages
Admission: Children under age 2 free; Kids 2-12 $7; Adults $10; Senior citizens $8.50
Physical location: 7705 FM 362 in Brookshire
Call for directions or see the map online.
www.dewberryfarm.com 866-908-FARM (866-908- 3276)
How would you rate this? ☐ ☐

▓ Despite their recycling potential, thousands of aluminum cans end up in the world's landfills. But kids who save their aluminum soft drink cans will make a difference for the environment and zoo animals when they participate in **Cans for Critters** at the Houston Zoo. When kids under 12 bring their empty aluminum cans to the zoo during the first weekend in November, they'll receive FREE admission for that day.

Recommended age: 1+ years

Admission: Free with aluminum cans

Physical location: 1513 N. MacGregor

www.houstonzoo.org 713-533-6500 Please call for more details.

How would you rate this? ☐ ☐

▓ With the Indians playing an important role in the tradition of Thanksgiving, consider how much your children know about Indians today. The **Alabama-Coushatta Indian Reservation** in Woodville (north of Houston) offers group tours of a real Indian reservation. A visit here is sure to spark conversations about the differences between how Native Americans live today and long ago. You'll spend a lot of time outdoors so dress warm and bring a coat. This is a fun activity for classes or extracurricular activity groups.

Recommended age: 5+ years

Admission: $3/person

Physical location: U.S 190 East, 571 State Park Road 56 in Livingston

www.alabama-coushatta.com/ 936-563-1329

How would you rate this? ☐ ☐

▓ Visit Houston's **Arboretum** to see nature flourishing in the midst of a bustling city. Take a walk on the five-mile track as you peer into critters' natural habitats. The Nature Center building also offers interactive exhibits to teach children about the outdoors in an enjoyable way. Various classes are also available for kids age 3-5 and 5-12. Please call the Arboretum for details.

Recommended age: All ages

Admission: Exploring on your own is free. Classes range in price from $12-$15.

Physical location: 4501 Woodway Dr. within Memorial Park

www.houstonarboretum.org/ 713-681-8433

How would you rate this? ☐ ☐

11/18 - 1/7: Moody Gardens features the **Festival of Lights.** Bring the entire family to view acres of lights and holiday music. Grab a pair of ice skates and glide across the outdoor ice rink, too. Santa Claus often visits the festival, so be good! Moody Gardens is open Christmas Eve and Christmas Day.

Recommended age: All ages

Admission: $6 per person with free admission for children under 3.

Physical location: 1 Hope Blvd. in Galveston

www.moodygardens.com 800-582-4673

How would you rate this?

11/23: The evening of Thanksgiving, the City of Houston kicks off the holiday season in grand style with the **lighting of S. Post Oak Boulevard** in the Galleria area. Fun for the entire family, Houston lights its outdoor Christmas trees and decorations to turn bustling blocks into glistening gems. Typical features include performances by local choruses, brief reenactments from the Houston Ballet's Nutcracker, and a fireworks display to conclude the evening. Parents can purchase hot cocoa and cider from some of the nearby hotels. Children love the holiday souvenirs that vendors sell on the street. And, of course, Santa makes an appearance as well. This is an all-time family favorite.

Recommended age: all ages

Admission: Free

Physical location: S. Post Oak Boulevard (between San Felipe and Westheimer)

www.houstontx.gov

How would you rate this?

Late November through December: **Houston Ballet** presents **The Nutcracker** each holiday season and it's another wonderful way to kick off the holidays. Children love the flying bakers, dancing sweets and snow-filled scenes. Adults can explain the story before the performance begins so youngsters understand the unfolding tale. Arrive early to be seated.

Recommended age: 5+ years

Admission: Tickets begin at $22

Physical location: Brown Theater at Wortham Theater Center at 501 Texas Avenue near Smith St.

www.houstonballet.org 713-523-6300

How would you rate this?

■ Each year on the Friday following Thanksgiving, families can enjoy a free day at the **Houston Zoo!** Plus, it's a great way to walk off all the turkey and treats!
Recommended age: 1+ years
Admission: None today
Physical location: 1513 N. MacGregor

www.houstonzoo.org 713-533-6500
How would you rate this? ☐ ☐

■ **Seasons of Sharing** runs at the Children's Museum of Houston from November through December. This annual exhibit celebrates Kwanzaa, Ramadan, Diwali, Christmas, Las Posadas, Hanukkah, and Lunar New Year. This gives children a chance to learn about holidays that others celebrate.
Recommended age: 3+ years

Admission: $5; Thursdays 5-8 p.m. are free; $3 Tuesday – Sunday 3-5 p.m.
Physical location: 1500 Binz in the Museum District
www.cmhouston.org 713-522-1138
Note: Open Tuesday - Saturday 9 a.m.- 5 p.m.; Sunday noon - 5 p.m. Only open on Mondays (9 a.m.- 5 p.m.) during the summer and federal holidays.
How would you rate this? ☐ ☐

December 2006:

■ 12/2 – 12/3: **Dickens on the Strand** is Galveston's return to the era of Charles Dickens and is a neat holiday activity. Families can walk the 10-block area in Galveston to see how characters from Dickens' stories lived. Costumed vendors and performers stroll about to entertain all. Children's activities include visiting the Royal Menagerie Petting Zoo, taking a ride on a pony and an elephant, playing in the "Snow on Sunday," joining in the Scrooge's Scavenger Hunt, hearing a storyteller, participating in a Backyard Circus and joining in the Puppet Parade as well as crafts and other projects.
Recommended age: 1+ years; Strollers are welcome.

Admission: Adult tickets are $10 in advance and $12 at the gate. Children age 7 -12 are $4 in advance and $6 at the gate. Children under 6 are free. Attendees dressed in full Victorian costume are admitted free.
Physical location: the Strand National Historic Landmark District in Galveston
www.dickensonthestrand.org 409-765-7834
How would you rate this? ☐ ☐

12/10: The Houston Symphony plays **Holidays Around the World** and is a charming way to spend a morning as a family during the holidays. Choose either the 10 a.m. or 11:30 a.m. performance. Youngsters can participate in arts and crafts before and after the children's show. Enjoy the performance with music from the Ukraine, Israel, Mexico and the United States. The performance usually includes singing, dancing, costumes and a visit from Santa.

Recommended age: 4-10 years
Admission: Adults $15; Children $9
Physical location: courtyard level of Jones Hall at 615 Louisiana St. in downtown
www.houstonsymphony.org/education 713-224-7575
How would you rate this?

There's just nothing like packing the car full of kids, blankets and hot cocoa to drive around town looking at **holiday lights.** Local TV news stations usually highlight some extra bright neighborhoods. Two favorite neighborhoods are **Shepherd Park Plaza** and **Candlelight Plaza** that have holiday-themed streets. (Take 6-10 north and exit Ella. Head north on Ella and turn right on one of the many streets entering the neighborhood.) The **Heights** also has festive lights. Sing carols and don't forget the candy canes.

Recommended age: All ages
Admission: None
Physical location: Neighborhoods throughout Houston
How would you rate this?

Count your blessings. No matter what your race or religion, all of us can recognize how blessed we are. This holiday season, **give back to your community** by encouraging children to participate in the giving (not just receiving). Children can do extra chores to earn money to donate to the Salvation Army collection spots around town. Load up some nonperishable goods and take them to the Houston Food Bank so that others have plenty of food this season. Do a good deed just to help another and reap the reward of knowing you made someone else feel special.

Recommended age: 1+ years
Admission: Free
Physical location: various donation locations throughout Houston
www.salvationarmyhouston.org/ 713-752-0677;
www.houstonfoodbank.org/ 713-223-3700
How would you rate this?

- The 5th Annual Spirit of Texas Toy Drive kicks off on T
runs through mid-December, benefiting the Salvatior
Recommended age: 1+ years
Admission: Free
*Physical location: Donations can be dropped-off at KHC
Casa Olè restuarants, and Keller Williams Realty locatioı*
www.khou.com/community
How would you rate this? ☐ ☐

A candlelight Christmas is available at **Washington on the Brazos** State Historical Site in Washington (about an hour drive northwest of Houston). Hear stories of Christmas customs and traditions celebrated in 19th century Texas. Enjoy music, carols, arts and crafts to take home, buggy rides. You can even decorate the historic house for the holiday.
Recommended age: 1+ year

Admission: Adults $6; Children $4
Note: At the time of publication, the 2006 date had not been set. Call for details.
Physical location: 12300 Park Road 12 in Washington, Texas
www.birthplaceoftexas.com 936-878-2213
How would you rate this? ☐ ☐

A young artist in bloom? **The Mad Potter** offers children (and adults) a chance to get creative by painting and customizing items such as dinner plates, ice cream bowls, banks (various shapes), figurines and more. Spend a few minutes choosing an item to decorate and then take an hour or two painting your work. The store will glaze and fire these creations for pick up later in the week. These also make great holiday gifts. All stores are open daily but hours of operation vary.
Recommended age: 5+ years
Admission: $8 per child painter + $8-$16 per pottery piece
Physical locations: The Mad Potter River Oaks at 1963-A West Gray; 713-807-8900
The Mad Potter West at 1341 S. Voss Rd.; 713-278-7300
The Mad Potter Bellaire at 4882 Beechnut at 6-10; 713-664-8808
The Mad Potter Sugar Land at 4787 Sweetwater at Highway 59; 281-313-0555
www.themadpotter.com ☐ ☐
How would you rate this?

CONTACT US

To recommend an event or activity for future editions of
100+ ACTIVITIES for Houston Kids , please e-mail the details to
KidsInfo@houston.rr.com
or visit:
MeganSalch.com.

Let me know your thoughts or suggestions on this book, too.

ADD YOUR OWN NOTES

"This book is great for newcomers and native Houstonians. It provides the insight to events that makes me feel like I have been there before."

"Finally, one concise place to find fun-filled activities suitable for the entire family."

–Stacey Wood, Houston mom

"Planning family-friendly outings with a preschooler in tow can be a challenge. A one-stop resource for ideas and event information is fabulous and very, very welcome!"

–Juli Crow, Houston mom